ALFRED's SACRED PERFORMER COLLECTIONS

Sunday Morning
Hymn Duet Companion

MW00862322

17 Familiar Hymns for One Piano, Four Hands

Arranged by Victor Labenske

What a joy it has been to write this 10th volume in my *Sunday Morning* series. Duets provide pianists with the opportunity to share the gift of music with an ensemble partner; and doing so to the glory of God makes this experience even more rewarding! The hymns in this collection were recently noted in a survey as the most commonly used hymns in hymnals over decades. It is my hope that you will be able to use these popular selections in *Sunday Morning Hymn Duet Companion* in many contexts, including church, recitals, and competitions. God bless you as you share your musical gifts for His glory.

Victor Labenske

A special thanks: I am grateful to my friends Kay Etheridge, Brenda Martin, Melva Morrison, Lisa Pagan, and Pam Yates who skillfully read through these arrangements and provided me with valuable input.

Copyright © 2018 by Alfred Music
All rights reserved.   Printed in U.S.A.
ISBN-10: 1-4706-3894-0
ISBN-13: 978-1-4706-3894-8

Alfred

Cover Image:
Stained Glass © Getty Images / BahadirTanriover

ALL HAIL THE POWER OF JESUS' NAME

SECONDO

Oliver Holden
Arr. Victor Labenske

Majestically (♩ = 120)

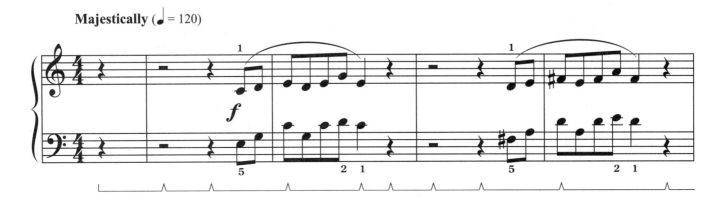

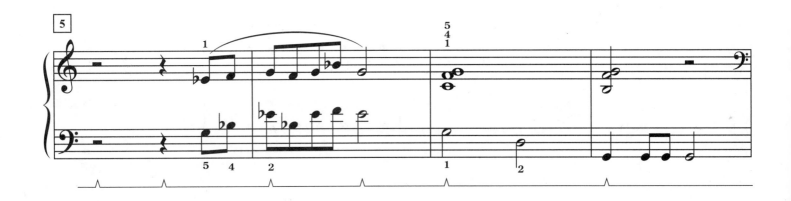

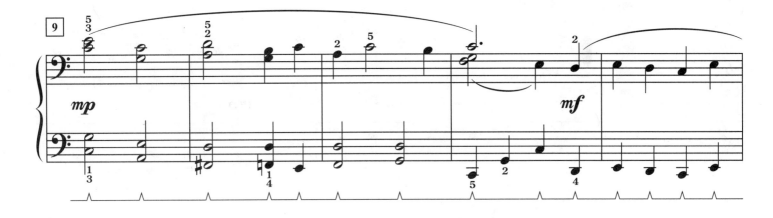

(Approx. Performance Time – 2:45)

ALL HAIL THE POWER OF JESUS' NAME

PRIMO

Oliver Holden
Arr. Victor Labenske

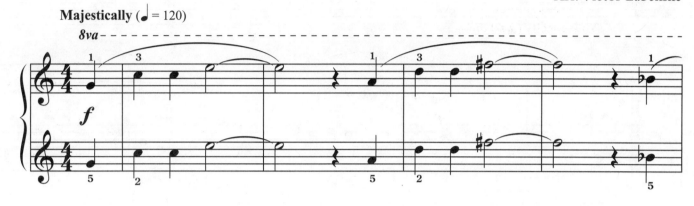

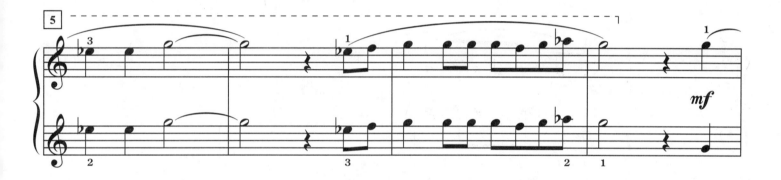

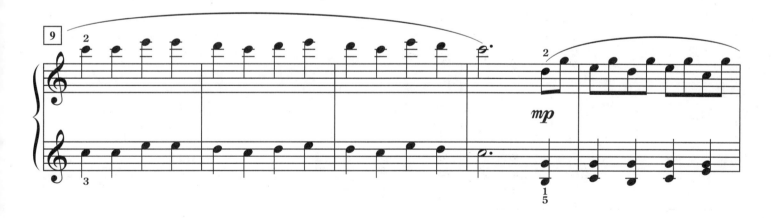

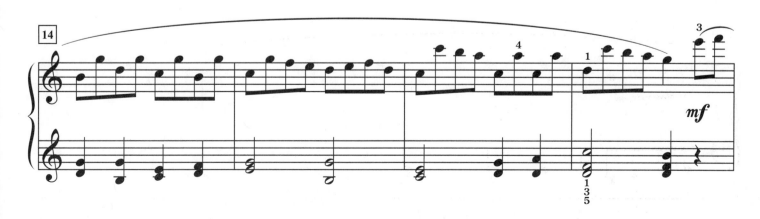

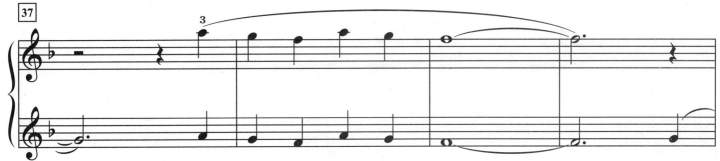

COME, THOU ALMIGHTY KING

SECONDO

Felice de Giardini
Arr. Victor Labenske

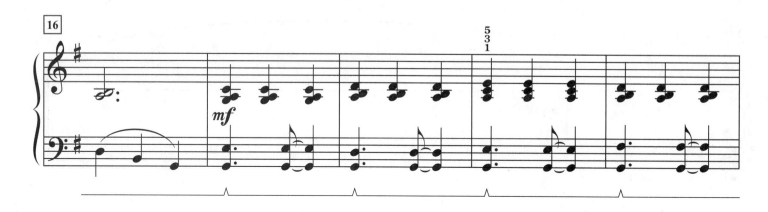

COME, THOU ALMIGHTY KING

PRIMO

Felice de Giardini
Arr. Victor Labenske

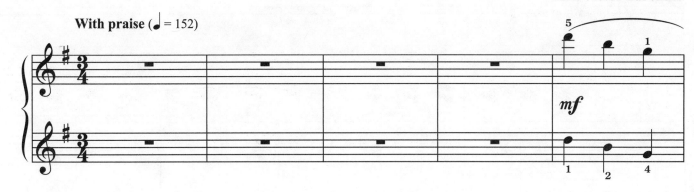

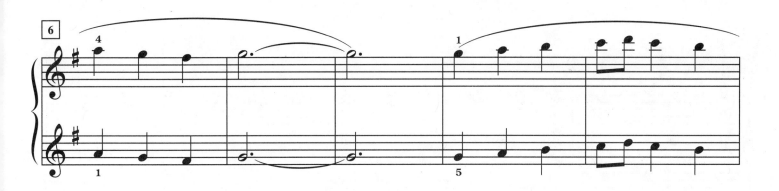

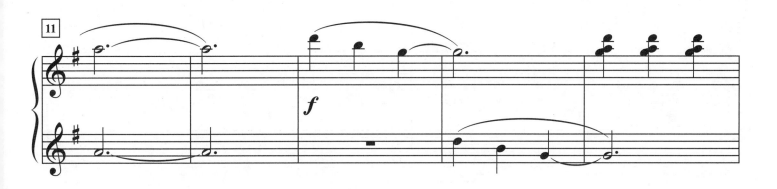

COME, YE THANKFUL PEOPLE, COME

SECONDO

George J. Elvey
Arr. Victor Labenske

COME, YE THANKFUL PEOPLE, COME

PRIMO

George J. Elvey
Arr. Victor Labenske

CROWN HIM WITH MANY CROWNS

SECONDO

George J. Elvey
Arr. Victor Labenske

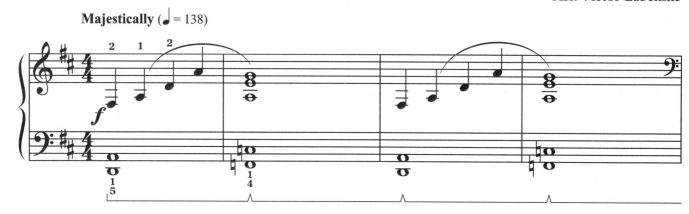

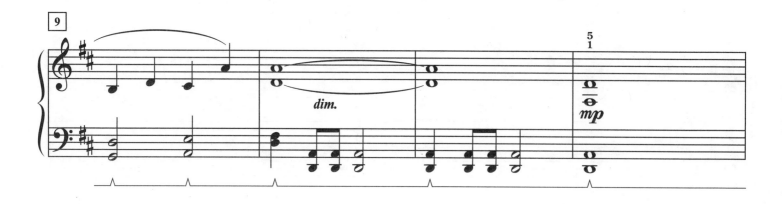

CROWN HIM WITH MANY CROWNS

PRIMO

George J. Elvey
Arr. Victor Labenske

Inspired by my son, Kristofer

GLORIOUS THINGS OF THEE ARE SPOKEN

SECONDO

Franz Joseph Haydn
Arr. Victor Labenske

(Approx. Performance Time – 2:00)

Inspired by my son, Kristofer

GLORIOUS THINGS OF THEE ARE SPOKEN

PRIMO

Franz Joseph Haydn
Arr. Victor Labenske

Guide Me, O Thou Great Jehovah

SECONDO

John Hughes
Arr. Victor Labenske

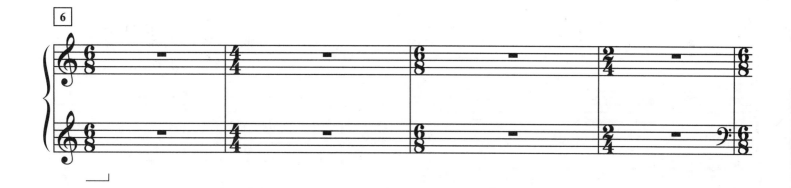

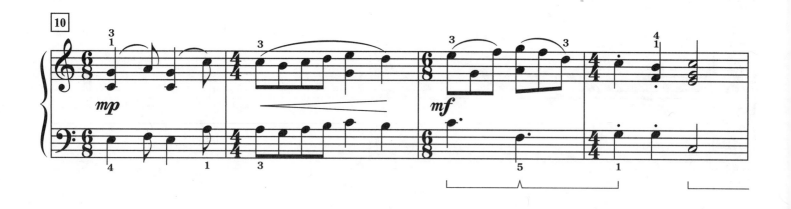

GUIDE ME, O THOU GREAT JEHOVAH

PRIMO

John Hughes
Arr. Victor Labenske

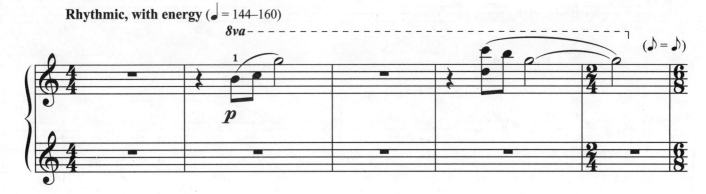

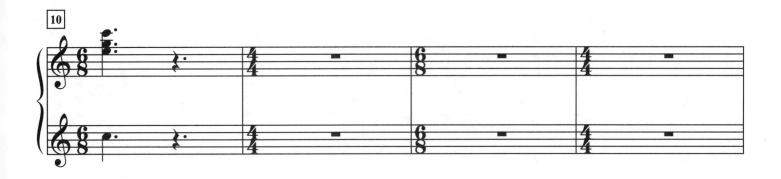

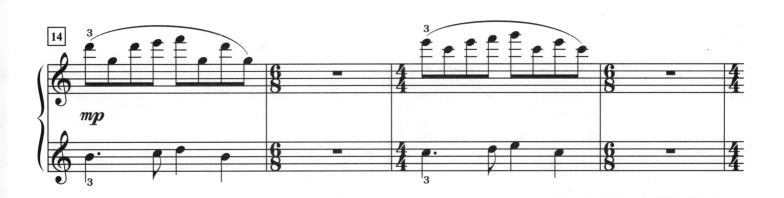

HOLY, HOLY, HOLY

SECONDO

John B. Dykes
Arr. Victor Labenske

(Approx. Performance Time – 2:30)

HOLY, HOLY, HOLY

PRIMO

John B. Dykes
Arr. Victor Labenske

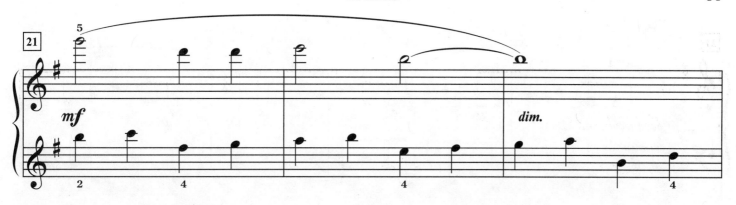

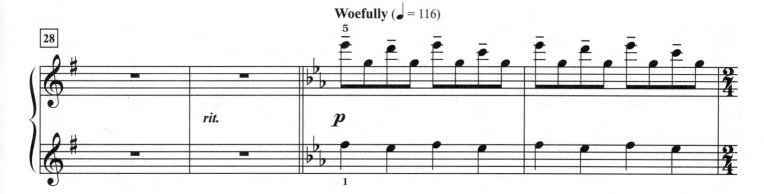

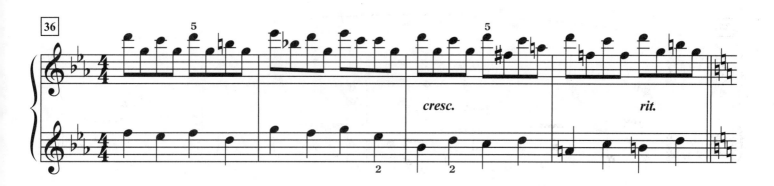

HOW FIRM A FOUNDATION

SECONDO

Traditional American Melody
Arr. Victor Labenske

How Firm a Foundation

PRIMO

Traditional American Melody
Arr. Victor Labenske

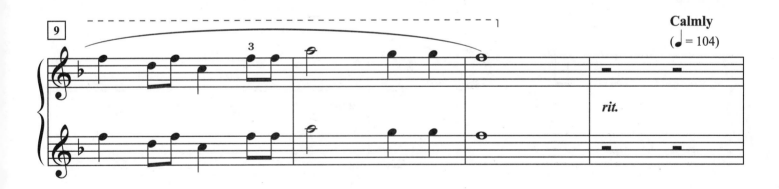

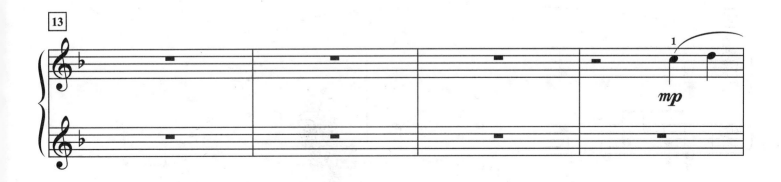

JESUS, THE VERY THOUGHT OF THEE

SECONDO

John B. Dykes
Arr. Victor Labenske

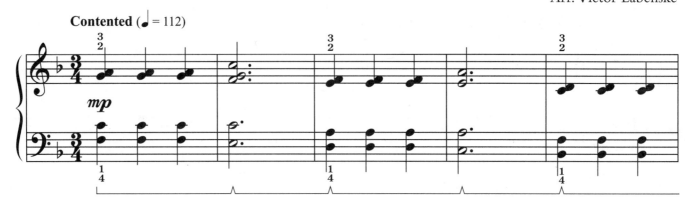

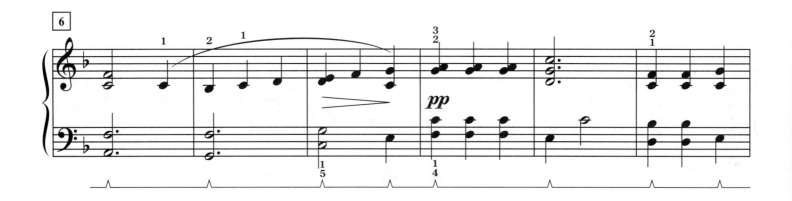

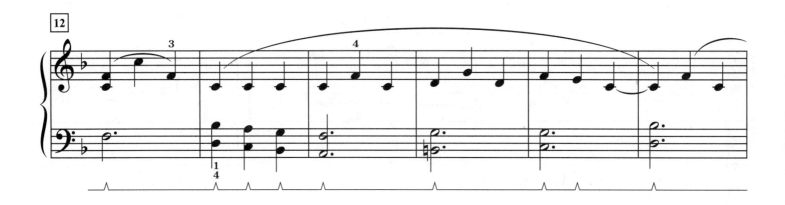

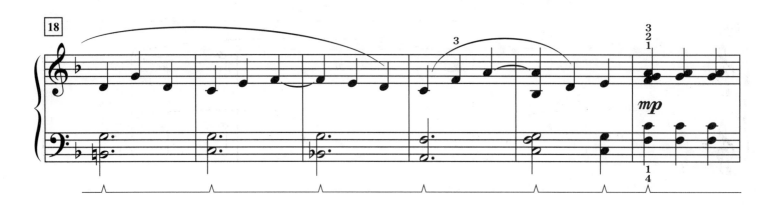

Jesus, the Very Thought of Thee

PRIMO

John B. Dykes
Arr. Victor Labenske

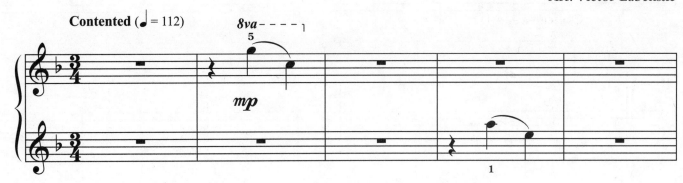

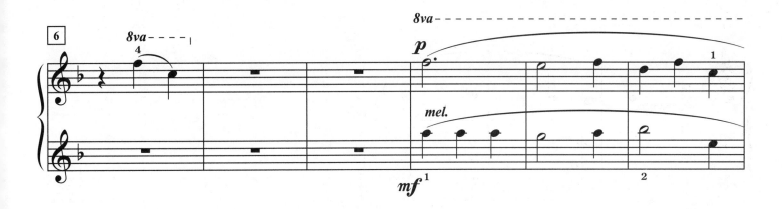

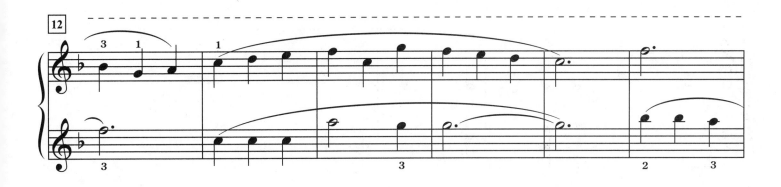

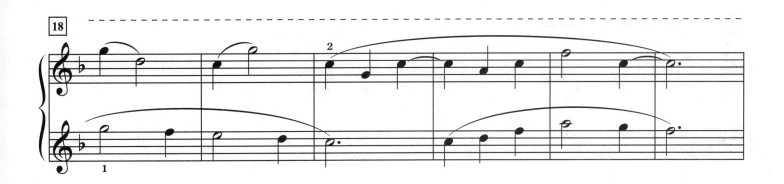

LOVE DIVINE, ALL LOVES EXCELLING

SECONDO

John Zundel
Arr. Victor Labenske

Enraptured, with great expression (♩ = 120)

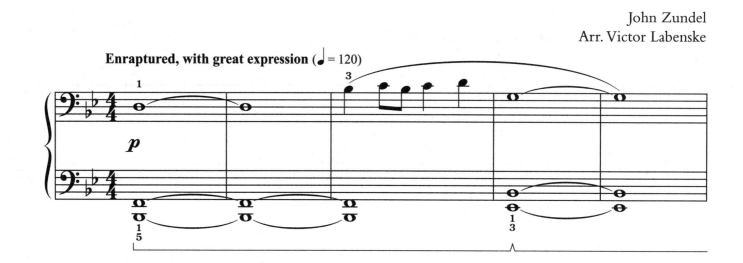

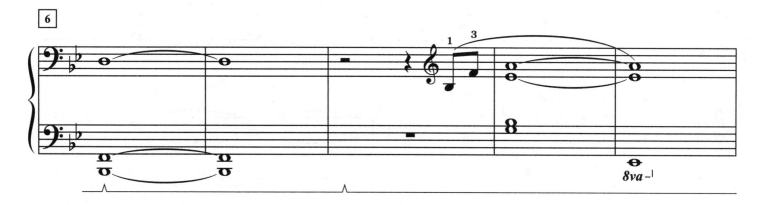

LOVE DIVINE, ALL LOVES EXCELLING

PRIMO

John Zundel
Arr. Victor Labenske

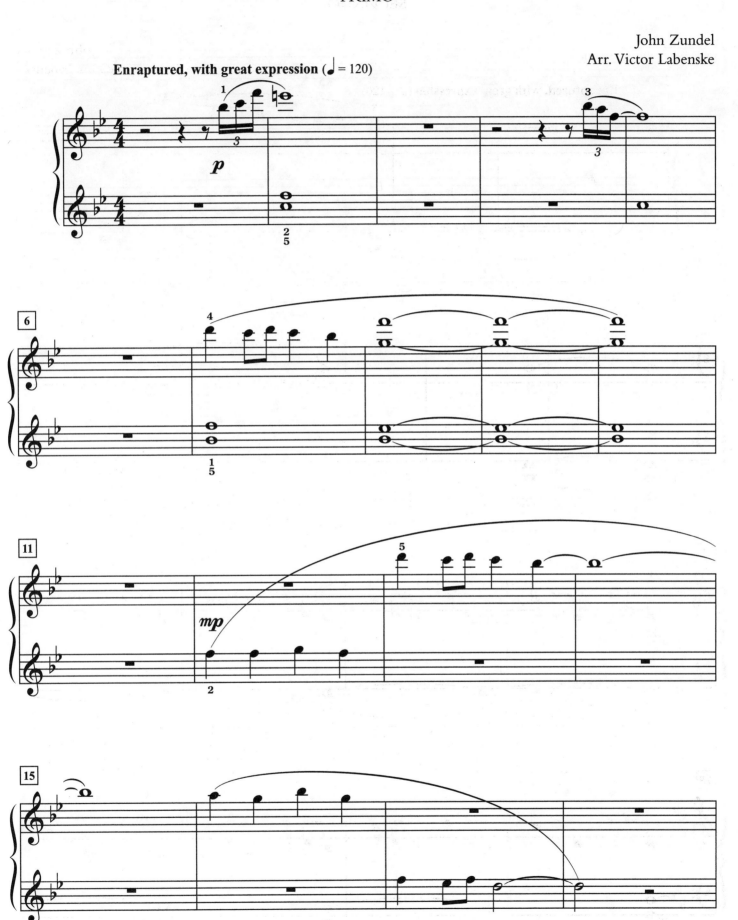

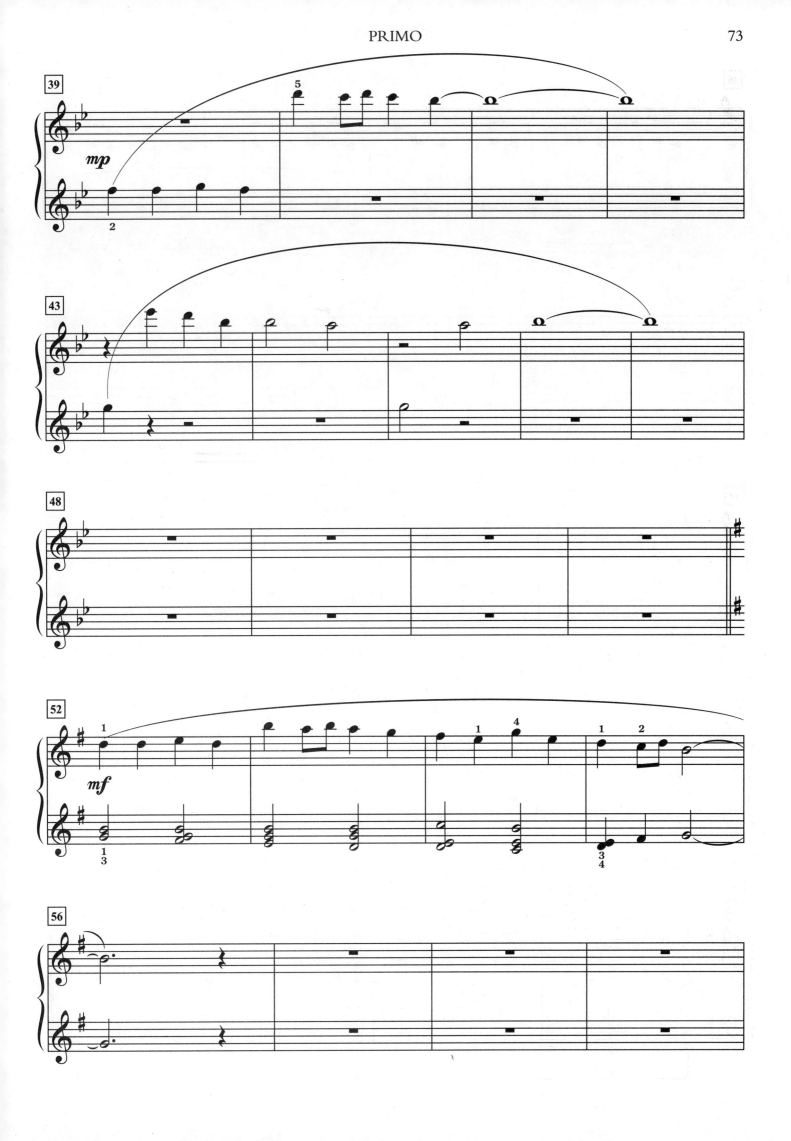

A Mighty Fortress Is Our God

SECONDO

Martin Luther
Arr. Victor Labenske

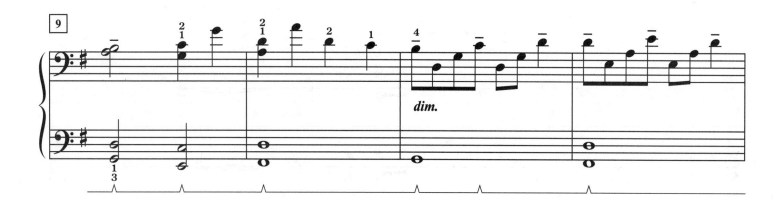

(Approx. Performance Time – 2:45)

A Mighty Fortress Is Our God

PRIMO

Martin Luther
Arr. Victor Labenske

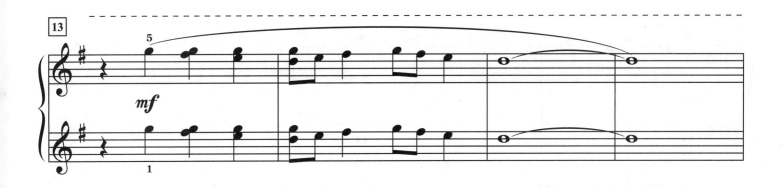

NOW THANK WE ALL OUR GOD

SECONDO

Johann Crüger
Arr. Victor Labenske

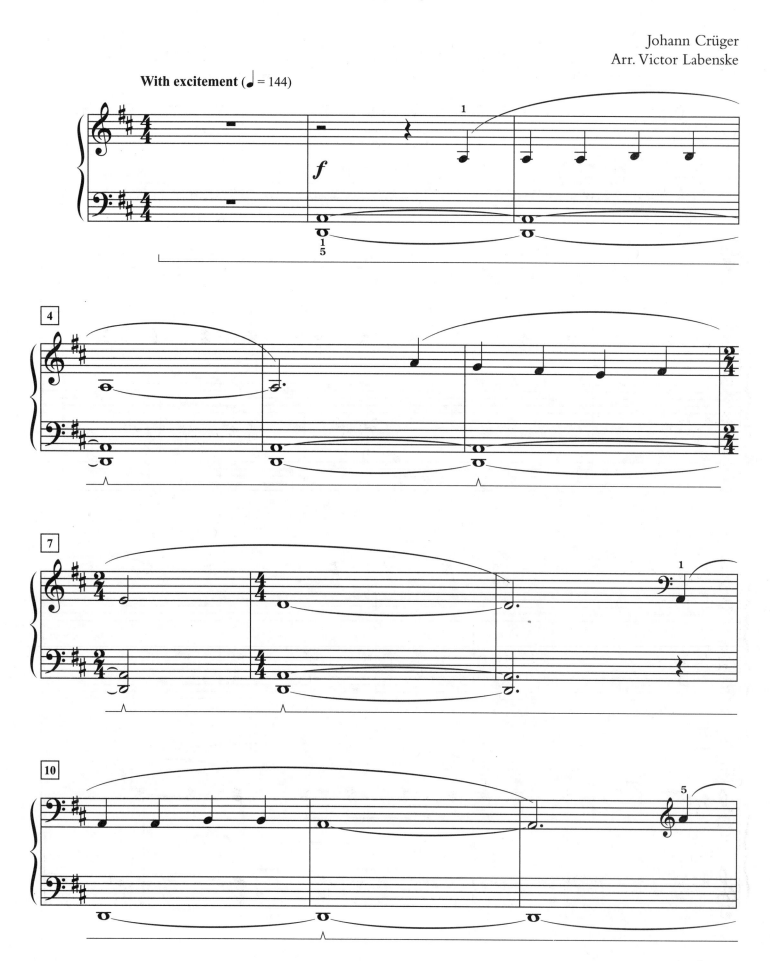

NOW THANK WE ALL OUR GOD

PRIMO

Johann Crüger
Arr. Victor Labenske

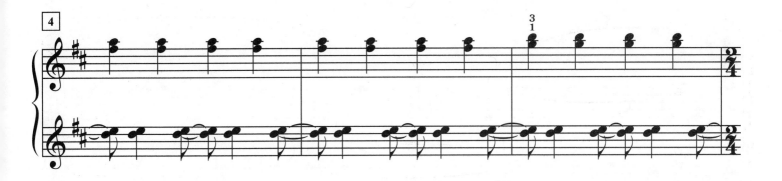

O for a Thousand Tongues to Sing

SECONDO

Carl G. Gläser
Arr. Victor Labenske

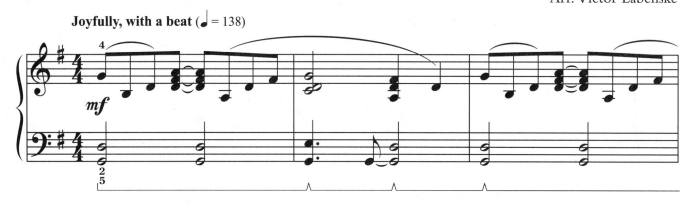

O for a Thousand Tongues to Sing

PRIMO

Carl G. Gläser
Arr. Victor Labenske

Joyfully, with a beat (♩ = 138)

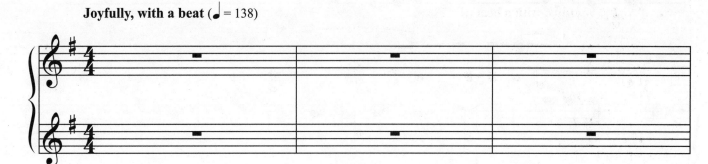

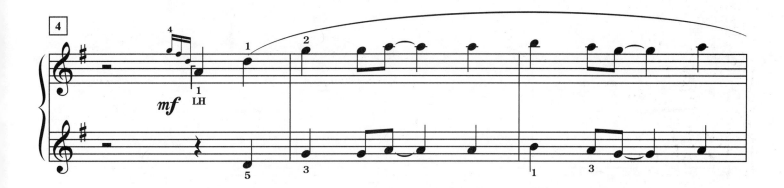

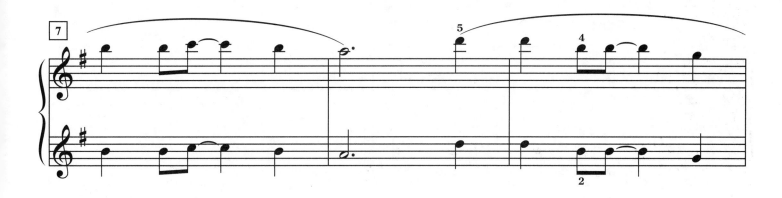

O God, Our Help in Ages Past

SECONDO

William Croft
Arr. Victor Labenske

Confidently (♩ = 126)

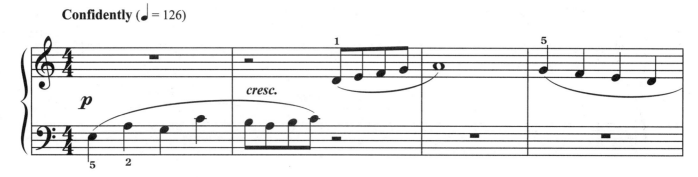

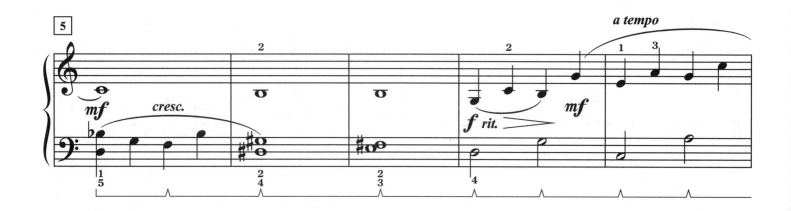

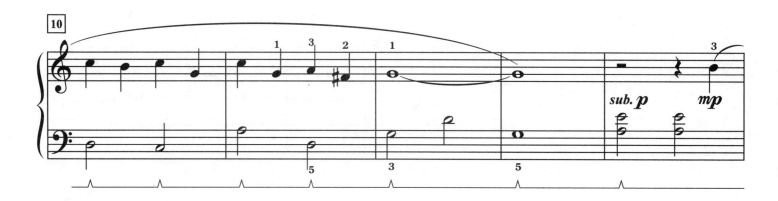

O God, Our Help in Ages Past

PRIMO

William Croft
Arr. Victor Labenske

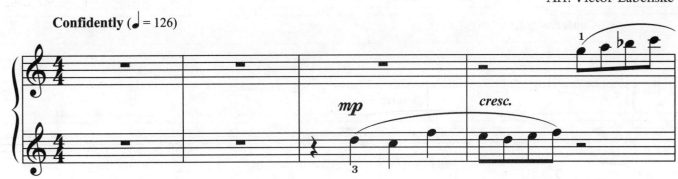

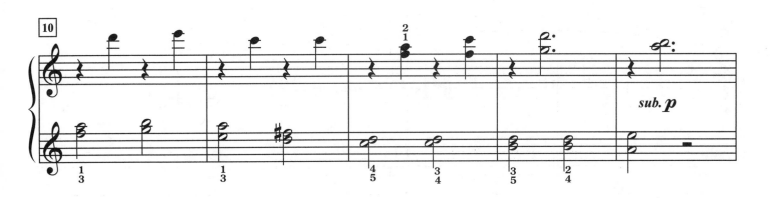

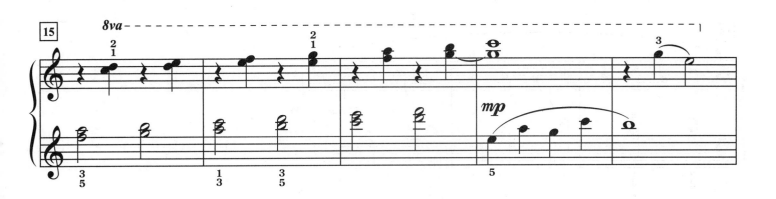

RH of secondo under
LH of primo

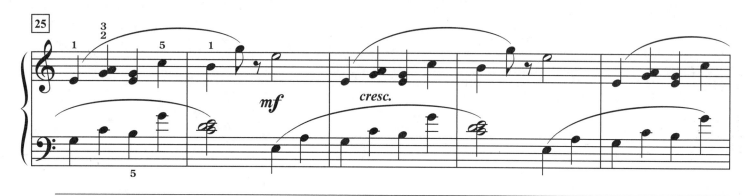

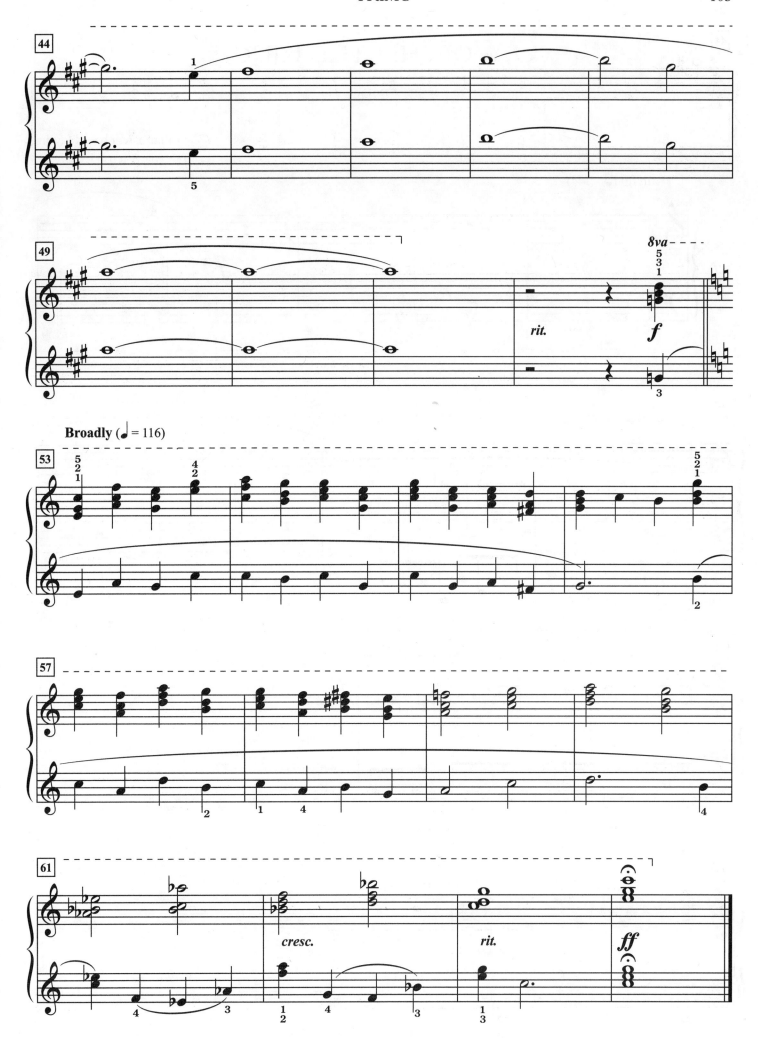

O WORSHIP THE KING

SECONDO

Johann Michael Haydn
Arr. Victor Labenske

Joyful (♩ = 144)

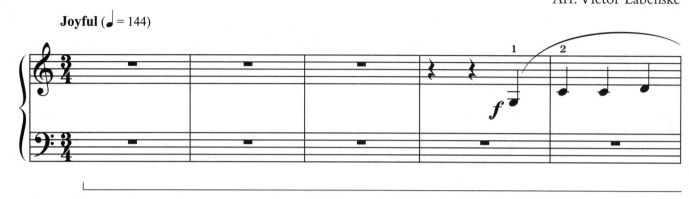

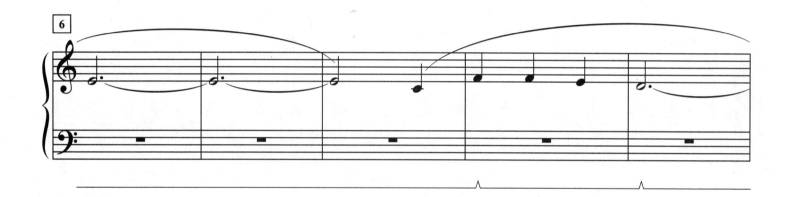

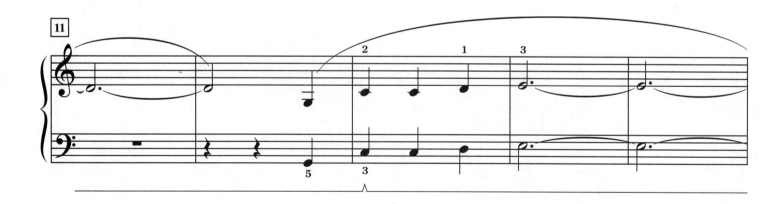

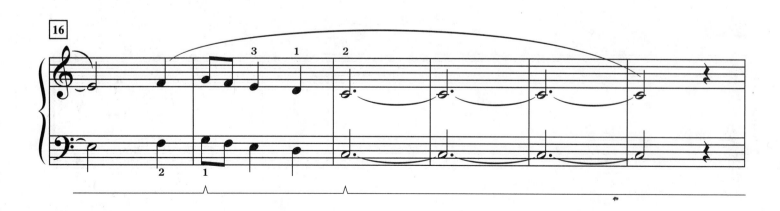

(Approx. Performance Time – 2:00)

O Worship the King

PRIMO

Johann Michael Haydn
Arr. Victor Labenske

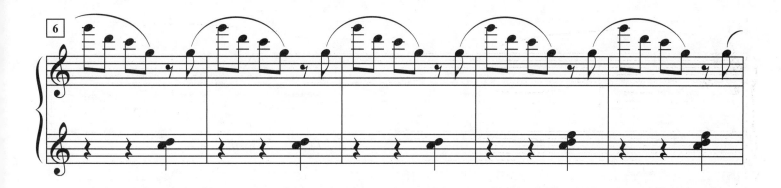

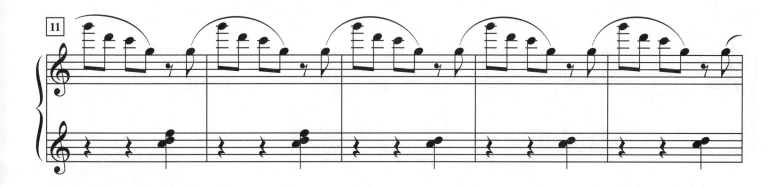

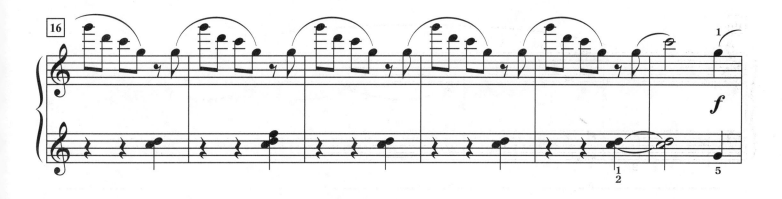

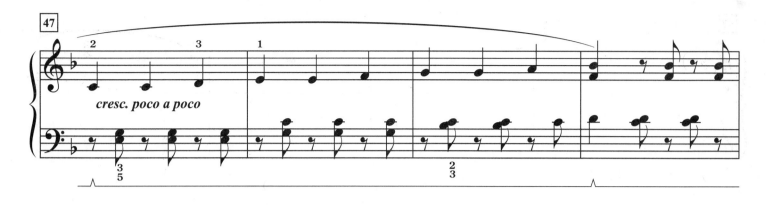

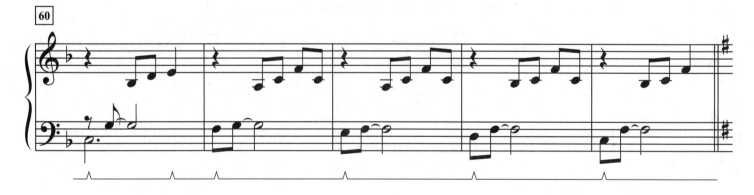

SAVIOR, LIKE A SHEPHERD LEAD US

SECONDO

William B. Bradbury
Arr. Victor Labenske

Savior, Like a Shepherd Lead Us

PRIMO

William B. Bradbury
Arr. Victor Labenske

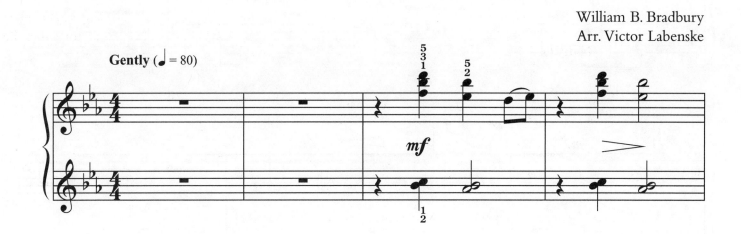

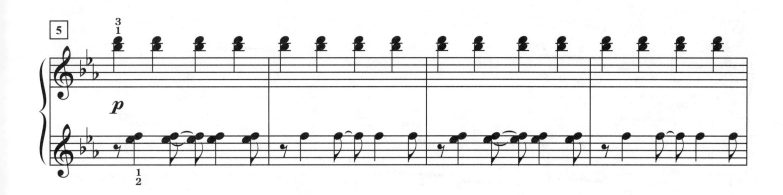

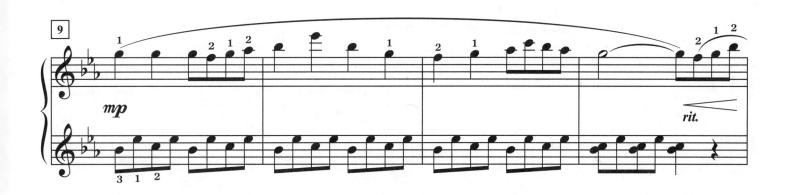

WHEN I SURVEY THE WONDROUS CROSS

SECONDO

Lowell Mason
Arr. Victor Labenske

Tenderly ($\quad$ = 112)

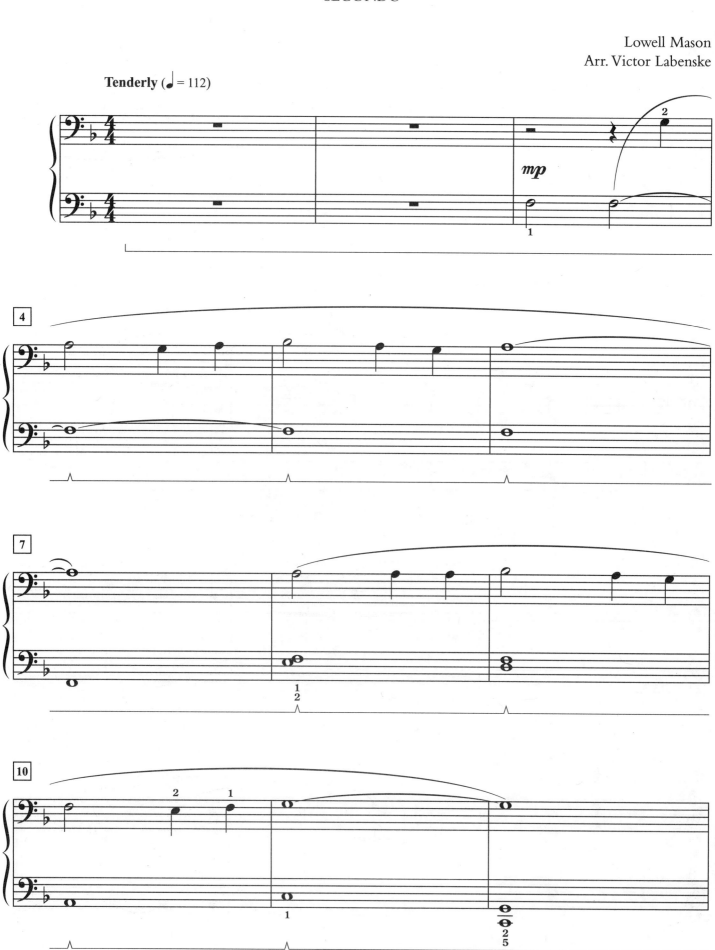

WHEN I SURVEY THE WONDROUS CROSS

PRIMO

Lowell Mason
Arr. Victor Labenske

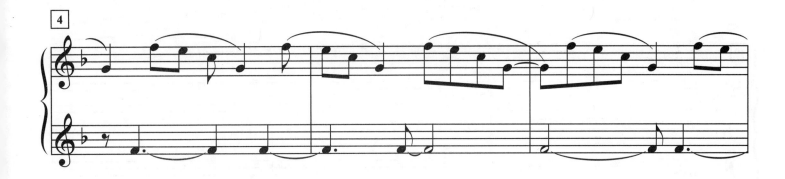

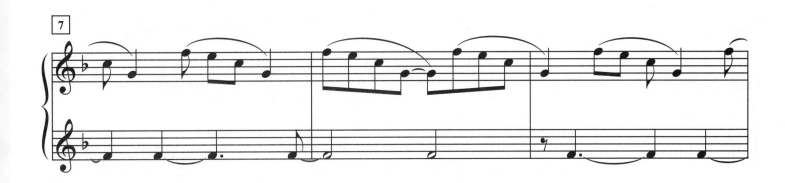

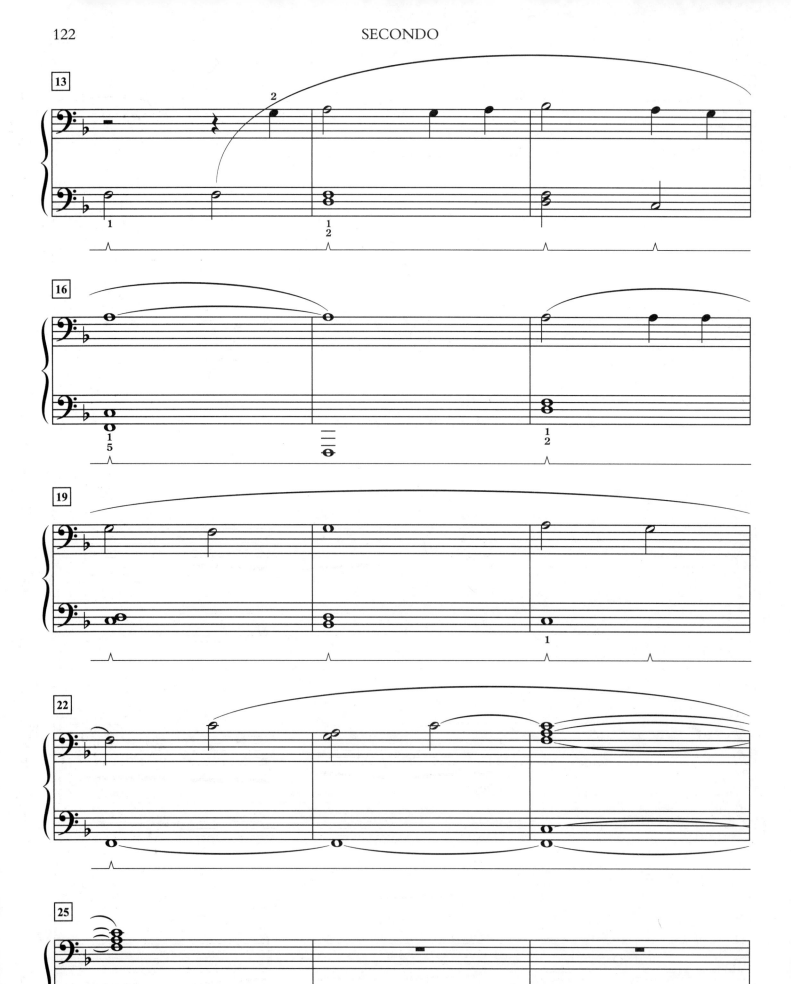